A STAFFORDSHIRE LASS

Leonora Slinn

to my parents, Leonora and James Slinn

With love to Glenys and Tony
from Barbara.

About the author

Leonora Slinn was born in Stafford and is proud to be part
of such a delightful and historic county. She has been
writing poetry from the age of seven and is pleased to share
her memories with you.

ISBN 978 184426 875 7

Published by printondemand-worldwide 2010

CONTENTS

1 Childhood and Schooldays

2 Living in the Country

3 Family

CHILDHOOD AND SCHOOLDAYS

Fear

I first felt fear at Rhyl,
aged five,
making sandpies,
hemmed in by waves
of people laughing, talking –
not *my* people –
mother was dead –
father had disappeared
suddenly …

Wildly searching with my eyes
he was not there!
I ran up sandy steps
across the road
down twists and turns of streets
in at the gate, the door
of the boarding house
into the haven of our room
and locked the door.

I was distraught!
I wept and wept.
A maid came running –
tried the door …
offered a banana –
cajoled, cried …
I kept it locked.

Father came, unbelieving,
hugged me tightly,
kissed me, comforted –
"I was there – right by you!
didn't you see me, love,
my little chick?"

2

incredulous that,
having lost me,
instinct had led me back
to safety's door.

God had given
my first sense of direction
and I had felt the first
sharp stab of fear.

From a Child's Bedroom Window

The Monday morning washing flaps aloft
row upon row as far as eye can see;
like lines of sailing ships the houses seem
lacking in only sea and pouting prow;
and when the washing's dry in the afternoon
and freshly-ironed garments hung to air,
white smoke will billow out from bright-lit fires
and steamers surge through gardens into night.

Izaak Walton Street

This is the street of my childhood ... my childhood,
of hot summer holidays' knickers and vest,
sitting on kerbstones with papers of sugar
and sticks of red rhubarb to dip in with zest.

A bicycling boy with fresh rolls every Sunday,
(and bells from Saint Mary's – but none from Saint Chad)
warm froth from the can into outstretching milk jugs
of neighbours, news-hungry, good tidings or bad;

Scrap carts and coal wagons and steaming horse-droppings,
Gran, framed in her pretty wisteria-ed door,
a flick of the shovel – then through to the garden
to feed the tea-roses she loved even more.

The dark little shop with its vinegar barrel,
gobstopper globes of tongue-sucking surprise,
black liquorice whirls ... oh how well I remember
a Saturday penny at Mrs. MacTighe's.

Young schooldays beginning, with skipping and topping,
hoop-bowling and marbles and hopscotching jigs;
then waiting for Gwenny, in warm winter 'vessy'.
imbibing with relish her Syrup of Figs!

Or Hazel, the daring, the awesome, inspiring,
hair flying, mouth smiling, with trippeting feet:
"Is your name Freddie? I'll kiss you! I'll kiss you!"
then chasing the boys to the end of the street.

Roads

You see this busy road, its bordering houses planned
with tasteful opulence? the starkly modern church,
the children's park and here and there a graceful lime?

When I was small, green fields enclosed a country road,
a farm, high hedges where my father pointed out
glow-worms before we reached the avenue of limes.

We'd walk to Warrens Lane to find the first white violet,
blue harebells nodding on the rabbit slopes,
and by the lodge a dog-rose, deepest pink of all;

Around the rambling bends to where damp meadows lay
golden with king-cups, mauve with ladies' smocks,
pink ragged robin – a lovely bunch for Gran,

And once a month I walked with her to take
church magazines to Betty Hatch (a row of cottages
hidden by flowers through a little wicket gate);

And then there was the road to daily school:
scattered with children, safe in twos or threes
to wander leisurely or wait, impatient, by some gate.

I ambled there with Mona, or with Gwen and Joan,
or sometimes with my aunt who came to stay
and startled me with red toe-nails and other London ways.

We carried tops and hoops, marbles and ropes and bits
of slate for hopscotch games; but there were two who had
thick boots and callipers and couldn't join the fun.

Tuesdays we took the road to Granny A's:
not busy then, but for the whizzing bicycles
and in the summer Guisso's trundling ice-cream cart;

She bought me jugs of it and packs of wafers too,
to make my own ice creams for crowds of friends
("My Gran'll have you") ushered in her little house.

There was the road that always led me back to home
from school, from friends or, Saturdays, the cinema –
haven of sweet escape with Dad, a wonderland!

With hoards of memories, what hosts of loved ones gone
people our roads! Houses may vanish – roads survive,
giving the spirits substance, strangely, in our dreams.

Aunt Jane

My Great-Aunt Jane was spinsterish
although she was married to Uncle;
they had no children but listened to
opera on the wireless:
indulging their fantasies in music
and carefully turned libretti.
Uncle did fire-drill in The War
while Auntie knitted for soldiers.

On previously planned excursions
my Aunt would come by omnibus
to take tea with my Grandmother –
a sisterly occasion.
I smelt her in the hallway
on my return from school:
a mixture of Ponds and mothballs
and primly starched virginity.

In later years my Grandmother,
in womanly confidences,
told me that Uncle had proposed
to her, when newly widowed;
(did she refuse from loyalty
or fear of an eighth confinement?).
So poor dear Aunt was second-best,
but Uncle was the loser.

They lie in a cemetery long unused
with a wood partition between them;
a neglected grave, a forgotten place,
a sterile end to a marriage.
Are they remembering celestial chords
or her heavenly home-made pastry?
Her hair in a bun with a mothball smell,
wry smile on his old grey-whiskered lip.

7

The Carol Service

Christmas congregations bring us together –
this year no snow, and the air so mild
that carols seem hardly in order –
the Staff sing lustily, loudly commanding us
'Hark to the Heralds! Adeste Fideles!'
boughs of green foliage tastefully mingled
with sprays of red berries.

The fir tree is lit by tiny wax candles,
the glow becoming a gradual gutter
entailing the ritual snuffing,
the careful replacement of fresh scarlet tapers.
'Unto us a Boy is born' –
rows of sad spinsters ardently praising
the birth pangs of Mary.

Their voices are high or painfully cracked,
masculine even and comically unsuited
to sing lullaby to a baby.
Can they concede that life has passed by them,
admit to themselves that war and their reticence
have robbed them of lovers?

Or is it in part their careful upbringing,
adherence to rules made for guiding young ladies
that made them so cautious towards men?
Purposeful Head, determined to mould us,
sings of a mayden that is makeless –
('aspire to her goodness and never ogle boys
on draughty street corners –
wear hats, gloves and stockings – do not chew in public,')

For their sakes I pray there will be a hereafter
where earth's bonds are loosened
and they can live freely without inhibition.
'Ding dong merrily on high' –
yet we, singing together each Christmas
are sitting by strangers.

Childhood

The scent of the earth in April
is sweet like our childhood past,
and glittering rainbow dewdrops
like treasures that we have lost.
Reflections of leaves at poolsides,
first flowers that linger on,
the fluting of birds in blossoms …
all echoes of hours long gone.
The warmth of the sun in April,
the gentle caressing air,
bring sounds of forgotten playmates –
don't turn, for they are not there.

Reminiscences of an Elderly Teacher

… and so we came on high-seated bicycles
or walked through the park on crisp Autumn mornings,
only a stone's throw from high-class lodgings,
to teach at a school for genteel young ladies.

Our days were the time-tabled disciplined hours,
the orderly days, months, (frighteningly) years
appropriate to dedicated mistresses;
if we prayed for change, the Lord never gave it.

The girls all married and brought their offspring,
with glowing faces, to grandchildren's parties.
'You never alter Miss A and Miss O –
your lives are eternal.' (like nuns in a convent).

At holiday time we gracefully vanished
to visit Mother and Father in Dorset;
or daringly booked a coach to the Continent
with a friend whom all the girls whispered was lesbian.

New members of Staff came who left to be married
and men were admitted to keep up the numbers;
the atmosphere changed, and somehow the Staffroom
was not quite the haven of peace that it once was.

And then Mother died and Father was ailing –
distressing arrangements made for his upkeep;
sadly the voices grow fainter and fainter,
too late now to ask them the meaning of life.

LIVING IN THE COUNTRY

On Choosing a Husband

A man whose land is over-neat
is not the sort I like to meet:
his weeds are hoed, his borders trim –
a proper niggle-werrit him!
Likewise a man I cannot bear
who leaves his tools out everywhere:
decayed with rust and flower-pots cracked
his mother spoiled him, that's a fact!
But one who lets his garden grow
as nature planned – a flower show
with bird and butterfly and bee
why – he's the one undoubtedly!

Heron

A heron visited the brook today,
shaped like a slender goose with stone-carved wing,
his steel-grey plumage startling and his eye
watchful and wary; with no sudden spring
he moved away across the green wet grass,
in silence dipped his head beneath the wire
and, stalking on his long grey stilts, soon passed
beyond the alders to a clearing where
I saw his massive wings unfold and stretch;
with steady beat he skimmed along the stream
and though I strained my eyes I could not catch
his flight, nor prove the substance of my dream.

Love and a Garden

We have been here at dawn and seen the morning mist
rise silently like smoke across the chill wet fields,
heard the green yaffle in the alder trees
laugh at our hopefulness – and fly away;
yet through the nettle patches and the tussocked grass
we saw a quick reflection of the rising sun…

We have been here at noon under the lilac trees' white blossom –
caught the rich sweetness of their scented breath –
glad of their dappled leaves in summer heat
to sit and marvel at the rainbow flowers,
the nectar-sucking butterflies and bumble bees
and new-hatched orange ladybirds on green glossed leaves.

And when we come again at dusk with fluttering moths,
walk with linked hands across the purple-shadowed grass,
do not be startled if you see our shades
lovingly bend to yellow evening flowers,
touch all their petals with a light caressing hand
and turn to smile at pipistrelles' soft swooping wings.

We made this garden once with full and loving hearts
for children's feet to play and turtle doves to sing;
we planned the paths and planted shrubs and trees,
entwined the roses, coaxed the fruit and herbs,
because we know one day, down where the water flows,
the woodpecker will come again – and you will hear!

Summer Idyll

There is no hint of war …
the questing bee explores the cavern of the paeony,
while other members of his family
murmur beneath the rhododendron.

Tall spikes of lupin flower on,
and summer marvels at their marathon:
can the new buds above see withered flowers
already gone?

These are the golden hours,
the windborne scent heavy with flowering bent;
whose senses keen enough to hear the lament
from fast-fading Hiroshima?

Summer Mirage

Did scented wallflowers bank the old flagged path,
forget-me-nots in riotous sprinkled blue,
lavender, cranesbill and red bergamot,
columbine heads with pink and purple wings,
herb-heavy drifts of sage and lemon balm,
marjoram, mint and clustered small-leaved thyme?

Did windows gaze on waves of poppied pink,
bee-buzzing thistles, striped and ribboned grass,
bell-flowers in season, daisies all the year –
mauve ones at Michaelmas, veiled with butterflies?
Summer brings visions of forgotten flowers
and vanished walls return in her mirage.

Midnight

We stood, and felt the witching hour
around us like a curtain fall –
the frozen fields, the icy air,
the vixen's chilling, eerie call,
the moonlit cattle by the hedge,
the shadows on the silent grass,
the twisted, silhouetted trees –
they knew it fell,
they felt it pass.

All movement ceased – no rabbit cowered,
no rustling mouse with frightened eye,
no beetle stirred nor prick-eared hare,
no barn-owl cleaved the midnight sky –
from spinnied hill to frost-rimed sedge
all living creatures held their breath,
the candle-leaved eternal trees
stood motionless
as though in death.

February Field

Grasses beside the stream stand dry and still,
caught in a frame of time by wintry cold
as if an unseen camera had paused –
invisible equipment ceased to film
in air sharp, sparse, and east-wind honed

And water – hard, cracked, brittle-boned –
freezes in flow, where devious twisted fold-
-upon-fold of draped and drifted snow has curved
in covering sheets above the dark stream's bed;
the sky is stark, swelling with silent sound.

Two startled snipe rise from the snow-blown ground
in starving unison; a kingfisher
skims with a flash of unexpected blue
to boomerang away and back again;
but old grey heron lies in feathered heap,
his "Frank! Frank!" greeting frozen in his craw:

Too late his rescue by the coming thaw
as water streams again through caverned snow;
pungent fox scent pervades the muck-strewn field,
and through white cloth of silver, diamond flecked,
green grass, glass-tissued, sparkles down the hill.

Tel: 0154 3. 417. 458

Dear Tony,

I've had a Christmas card from Maz today and she tells me that you are in hospital — I'm <u>so</u> sorry, and have put you on my prayer list, praying that you will soon make a good recovery. Perhaps Glenys will give me a ring to let me know how you are going on.

I've been meaning to send you the enclosed poetry book for some time, and hope you will enjoy it. The cover is a photo taken in our rose border at Horsley, when I was about 35! My pen-name is my

mother's married name. She died of TB when she was 23 and I was 2½ - so I can't remember her at all. The book is an autobiography in a way and there are two references to Granny Allen. "Roads" - page 6 and "Traffic Jam" page 53

Get well soon!

With love,
Barbara

Cobweb

Between the barbs of wire,
the moss-grown rail
beaded with drops
of iridescent mist,
netted with thread
finer than Orpheus' lyre,
the cobweb swells
its full September sail.

Discovery

Leaf after leaf this hawthorn cloaks the ground with crisp,
    dry brown,
and neither frosted chill nor bone-bite wind can pierce
    the soil.
Who finds this place in Spring and probes the mould with
    fingertips
will find the small splayed leaves, delicate stems, of
    moschatel.
Wonderment grows to see the green, mysterious five-side
    flowers.
Some call this miracle in miniature the 'town hall clock':
four faces point to each prevailing wind, and one to heaven.

Fox Paths

Bending and twisting through thick Summer grasses the trail
　　is erratic:
ryegrass and cocksfoot and short crested-dogstail ripple
　　in unison,
catstail and fiorin, tall meadow softgrass shed their fine
　　pollen
on cool secret tunnels, on still airless mornings.

Past high herif hedges and fat hogweed bursting to canopied
　　splendour,
and bell-spires of foxglove already reverting to green-cup
　　old age;
by wiry-stemmed nightshade whose purple flowers promise
　　blood berries to come,
the paths cross and criss-cross unseen but all-seeing.

In heat of the noonday, with yellow eyes narrowed against
　　the bright sun,
a vixen outstretches with tongue-lolling panting to watch her
　　cubs playing:
like children they dart and start, learning their cunning in
　　zig-zag confusion,
scattering feathers and dry bleaching bones.

In summers long gone the poor cottage children sauntered to
　　school
along these same by-ways: collecting all feathers, examining
　　bones,
day-dreaming, carefree, naïve and yet knowing the nest of
　　each robin,
the flight of the heron, the scent of the fox.

Hiding with bated breath round the warm haycocks,
   pouncing with joy:
shrieking to feel the ripe seed-heads of barleygrass climbing
   their sleeves:
counting the molehills where partridge had dusted, and
   naming each flower
each leaf and grey tree-shape as Autumn approached.

Distant, demanding, on white Winter mornings the old
   school bell called them,
ambling in twos and threes: sometimes a laggard panting,
   chest rasping
in breath-freezing air – and one, a small waif, dead in a
   snow tunnel,
fresh fox-prints the guide to discovery there.

Detection

There was a slight marking in the Spring corn,
a bending of green blades –
it could have been the wind's direction
but south winds bring their balm, their fragrance seeps
gently into the soul and does not have the power
for even a casual indentation – a mere suggestion of a track.

Day after day follow the course with the eye –
strength of feeling gripping –
meander cautiously down to the brook –
is there a hollow within the hedge?
continuation of purpose across the stream?
is it imagination?

Come rain and mud – daily detection grows –
definite slide marks down the bank,
possible pad-marks by the water –
the dog dwells more than a passing minute
on scents fresh, new and sharply exciting.

Heat of summer scorches the yellowing field,
hardens the cow-dung pats:
one day finds them tilted, tipped,
with snuffle marks in their under-softness
for beetles, worms, for maggots – juicier sustenance?

There comes to all enquiring minds some firm conclusion –
a stopping in the track –
footsteps take a new direction –
a slow inspection of a different hedge
where hollowed pits lie hidden, carefully far from home,
where casual passers-by would not observe
newly-secreted droppings ...

'And have you seen the badgers?'

FAMILY

To Jamie

Such a busy day Daddy
such a busy day!
I've done a lot of work
and I've done a lot of play.
I've dug in the garden
and scrubbed on the floor,
I've played with my water toys
and painted the door.
I've helped make some pastry
and sat on Mummy's knee.
I'm so glad you're home Daddy –
come and talk to me!

First Day at School

 "I liked it at the school today
with games to play and books to borrow,
and Grandad came to take me home …
oh! … must I go again tomorrow?

The uniform is green and yellow,
worn by every little girl,
and Daddy asked an older one
to hold my hand … her name is Pearl.

He says that, now that I am five,
'Don't say Daddy or even Dad'
(because he teaches at the school)
but 'Mr. Went'. It makes me sad."

Guess

"Guess who is coming down with jewels in his hair?"
Stepping down the stairway like a conqueror,
flashing diamonds worn to make his subjects stare,
clothed in fine apparel is an Emperor!

Agate and sapphire crown him to perfection,
amethyst and emerald set in gold –
guess whom the mirror gives majestic reflection?
Our little brother who is five years old!

Thursday

There's no P.E. on Thursday afternoons –
he likes it then because
he doesn't have to stand and watch
'the others', agile, nimbly leaping,
swarming high heaven-hanging ropes
with animal delight –
tippling and curling over on the mat –
fearful for his turn when he will be
'the one' who doesn't quite …
tottering along on spindly legs
which won't climb ropes – he wonders how
they find so much enjoyment
in this dreaded physical display –
his brother used to climb right to the top
so why can't he?
his sister tippled on the mat
better than anyone. He wants to be
a poet or a gardener when he's grown –
that's why he'd rather be
alone and quietly reading in another room.

Suburban Gardens

Suburban gardens are composed
of straight suburban rows
of tulips and lobelia,
the upright standard rose;
the permanent white concrete path,
black tarmacadam drive
that sweeps around the rollered lawn
where flowering cherries thrive;

but every country garden should
be wild, and full of bees
lazily buzzing through the blooms
of pear and apple trees;
with cobbled paths – or brick – or flag
where thyme can creep at will,
sweet mignonette and alyssum
their heady perfume spill;

and every child should know the peace
that comes with country play,
the saunterings in country lanes
between the banks of may;
the bluebells and pink purslaine flowers
in thick Spring carpets spread,
the cuckoo calls – and dark green ways
where secret foxes tread.

and every man who loves his child,
or seeks for peace of mind,
should leave the city once awhile
and secret gardens find

where sound is merely rising wind
that sweeps the willows low –
and hours are bending grasses
where the snail of time creeps slow.

Flowers for the Children

The golden flowers that herald Spring
gleam in the March and April sun:
aconite, coltsfoot, daffodil –
treasures of great Hyperion –
and little varnished celandine,
spill from the store where riches shine.

But May comes dressed in virgin white,
carpets of daisies laid to tread,
with blossoms in her flowing hair
and gardens' summer snowflake spread;
the last narcissus' golden eye
watches the bridal month go by.

Against the blue, tall whitebells stir,
small stitchwort weaves a worthy gown;
along the lanes, most daintily,
a veil of Queen Anne's lace hangs down;
Jack-by-the-hedge stands tall and bright
to welcome May, the year's delight.

Droppings

I have a friend who always says to nephews and to nieces,
'Be careful where you put your feet – don't tread in horses'
faeces!'

As this expression lacks finesse it's seldom ever heard,
so Beatrice E. decreed that 'Job' would be a better word.

How much more tactful and refined to hear a parent ask,
'Now, have you done your job today? a necessary task!'

The fact that some folk study jobs is one of life's surprises,
but Natural History reveals there are all shapes and sizes:

a rabbit's jobs are hard and round like pellets flung at random;
a sheep's are similar, but large, and scattered with abandon.

You can't mistake a cow's pancake, for it is like no other –
a calf leaves dribbles since it lacks th'experience of its mother.

A fox's 'calling card' is black, left on the route it's been,
but badgers are like cats and make a neatly dug latrine.

'Bea' once found, by my front door, a little half-inch dropping:
'Toad's job!' she shrieked in great delight – 'How absolutely
topping!'

So do not wrinkle up your nose when jobs you're contemplating;
remember that researchers find the subject fascinating!

Family Album

They stand and look at us from photographs
eighty years on;
display with careful Victorian grace
their flat, controlled Victorian face –
Grandpapa's and Grandma's friends
in stiff Victorian clothes:
prim buttoned bodices hiding emotions,
tucks and lace and velvet waistcoats
hiding emotions of … who knows what
eighty years on?

Will someone look at us, captured in photographs,
eighty years hence?
beaming smiles and casual poses,
admiring views or pruning roses –
someone's great-grand-pop and mom
in a long-forgotten place?
Hot-pants, jeans and stark bikinis,
sunshine hats and coloured lenses
concealing heartaches best forgotten,
eighty years hence?

Save Their Souls

I saw a celandine today!
I had to stop and smile
and touch its small unopened cup
and welcome its return.

The hedgebanks change with every Spring
and men who do not know
how much we love the trees and flowers
slash, desecrate and burn.

Prayer's not enough to save the land –
yet have I any power
to influence unthinking men
and prove my deep concern?

I know my grandchildren will have
a need for food and home –
they'll also have a soul to feed
on forest, flower and fern.

And will there be a celandine
to make them stop and smile
and touch its golden shining flowers
and welcome its return?

Thomas

Hello Thomas! Give me a hug –
friendship warm as a 'bug-in-a rug'!

Everything you do is nice–
Dalek drawings – so precise.

Collecting coins and sorting shells,
Cubs and camping, ringing bells.

Computer games are thrilling too –
show your Grandma what to do.

Now you're ten you're growing fast –
not long before my height is passed!

Christmas Presents

William has just reached his teen years
and he's gentle, kind and good,
protective to his younger brothers,
respecting elders as he should;
fishing is his keenest hobby –
out all weathers by the stream,
so, two pairs of fishing mittens
and a book to help him dream.

Jemmy's cooked since he was seven,
two years baking bread for Mum –
spatula and whisk are ordered –
he's an expert now, by gum!
As he loves to light the fire –
taught by Dad to do it right –
a Santa candle would be fun
to give the table festive light.

Charlie lives each magic day
as someone 'not quite seven' can
in a world of knights and dragons,
speeding horse and strong-armed man;
so I think I'll write a letter
to the Saint who brings each toy,
asking for a shield and sword
to protect a fighting boy!

STAFFORDSHIRE COUNTRYSIDE

The Midlands

(a riposte to Hilaire Belloc)

At last my native Midlands
your praises can be sung –
who dares to call you sodden and unkind?
Too long the phrase has rankled
the unjust words have stung –
how little truth the poet stayed to find.

Come to the heart of England
deep in its country ways,
soft-rising hill and reed-reflecting mere;
curlew and lapwing calling,
proudly the grebe displays,
mallard and coot and heron shelter here.

Robins in country gardens,
cottages thatched with straw,
house-martins nesting underneath the eves;
thrilling the thrush at daybreak
opening his heart's full store,
mellow the spell the gold-billed blackbird weaves.

Daisies bloom in the meadow,
border the twisting lane,
hide under fronds of sweet vernal and brome;
mingling among the foxtails
buttercups catch the rain,
glowing like lamps to guide the badger home.

Fairies' clubs in the beechwoods,
lichens on hawthorns lie,
beneath the birches scarlet flycap grows

and from the dark fir forests –
whose black peaks probe the sky –
the stinkhorn's putrid smell offends the nose.

Up on the rolling moorlands –
heather and bracken swept –
fat black grouse are lekking in the dawn;
down in the mist-grey birchwoods
the fallow deer have crept,
soft-dappled doe and velvet-muzzled fawn.

Streams in their hidden places
gurgle through cress and fern,
secretly join and to the rivers race;
reed mace and drooping willows
cluster in every turn,
haunt of the brown-flecked trout and silver dace.

Carpets of wild white snowdrops
pattern the greenwood's floor,
relics of winters milder here than most:
seldom the thunder rumbles,
floods rise beyond the door,
far from the mountains, far from the savage coast.

Look up, my lovely Midlands!
no longer hang your head –
for I shall be your valiant knight-at-arms –
display your sunset blushes
and proudly, firmly tread
to gather all of England in your arms!

Hidden Gardens

They come each Sunday in the afternoon
to gaze across the February pool,
pick willow in the yellow April sun,
or picnic on some well-loved, flattened stone
outcropping from this slope behind the Mere.

Parking their car beside an iron rail –
where forty years ago they leaned their bikes –
they wander well-known pathways through the wood
or, dreaming, sit and watch bright bubbles rise,
light midges dance, the kingfisher appear.

You'll see them often when the trees turn gold,
when hedgerows hung with blackberries invite –
with small, shy smile they'll pass the time of day,
peep quickly through some well-used cottage gate,
pausing to praise the flowers another year.

You wonder where they live? The weekly 'bus,
that takes you for your shopping into town,
drives right beside their narrow terraced house –
almost at stretching distance the concealing door
guarding their hidden garden, flower-lined.

Away from rumbling roads, encroaching noise,
they mark their own straight furrow with a spade –
away from shrieking streetlights' dazzling glare
they feed the wandering hedgehog bowls of milk,
remember suckling calves they've left behind.

They feel for friendship in a village lane;
we search companionship in busy towns;
the printed signs direct and redirect
but the true boundaries are invisible,
hiding the hidden gardens of the mind.

Cannock Chase Silver Birches

I have seen such trees on plates
in Chinese patterns, blue on white,
their fine-drawn twigs and dappled leaves
tumbling in waterfall cascades,
their slender trunks like arching bows
captured in immobility.

This is a green and lonely place
among the hills where nightjars purr,
along the shadowed valleys where
a solitary woodcock rodes –
caught, by the summer evening glow
the birches' immortality.

I Know a Wood

I know a wood of strange and hidden flowers
growing in green, as in a sanctuary,
where light or cold East wind can hardly penetrate
and only cockerels, crowing distantly,
show that the dawn has come.

Go without footfall by the dark, still pool
and in a soundless reverie move now
to where Herb Paris, hosta-ribbed and round,
cups its proud quadrants – leave them concealed in green,
crushing no flowers under –

and pass Sweet Woodruff with her handmaid's shawl
fringing the wood: picking a sprig or two
carefully in your hand, take to your books
where – in the pages pressed – the scent of hay
will drift your senses and your thoughts away.

Peafield Covert

Let me show you England on this bright September morning
as Autumn's sun throws banded shadows low across the hill;
the barley has been harvested and straw bales stand in
   silhouette
like prehistoric vertebrae, gigantic, carved and still.

Let's climb the five-barred field gate where bramble sprays
   are swaying,
thick with small pink blossoms and berries sharply sweet –
green and red and ripening black they hang in thorny
   clusters
before the Devil spits on them and they're not fit to eat.

Tall hogweed lifts brown-seeded heads in splendid isolation,
the hedges hide late harebell flowers, a myriad spiders spin;
down by the stream, where dazzling meadows spread their
   emerald carpeting,
sparrows and starlings flock and feed until the sun goes in.

The trodden stubble crunches as we climb towards the
   covert –
crowned with dark green ancient oaks that spread along the
   rise;
look there, across the valley, where the morning mists are
   vanishing,
eternal hills flow endlessly to meet clear English skies.

Cauldon Low

Men came and slashed this rising ground
to quarry stone and use the land as theirs;
sweated to carve through Winter's ice …
yet they have lost, for earth can wait its time
patiently, secretly and without a sound.

Now, on their road, gold trefoil gleams,
plantain defies our feet tenaciously,
bedstraw and vetches slowly spread
their matted stalks until the track has gone,
the rutted way no longer what it seems.

Green-mantled slopes in Summer haze
rise like a mirage over scattered rocks –
purpose forgotten – crevice filled
with twayblade, cowslip, yellow cat's ear, and
with quaking grasses blown on West-wind days.

The enclosure suddenly opens wide
to quarried bowl purpled with self-heal, thyme,
pinnacled orchid – all revealed
as if the earth were ravenous for flowers,
the mutilated land had never died.

Coombes Valley

(to George & Edna Lovenbury)

What do I remember?
I remember the steepness of it –
the slithering, sliding, zig-zag footing,
breathless, laughing, downward
plunge of the slope;
and a sturdy bridge, hand-crafted,
washed away as the waters rose
swirling, savaging, tree-branch tearing,
powerful, painful and unstoppable
suck of the vortex.
The unbelievable peace that followed:
birdsong scattered through leaf and raindrop,
glittering, glowing, flower-encrusted
glade of enchantment –
Autumn's joy of scrunching leaves
to your loam-banked cottage –
squirrel sightings, nut-husks, ink-caps
and your painting of fly-agaric.
We remember the tales you told
of Winter nights by the old coke stove;
music, lamplight, conversation,
warmth – the badger's sudden scratching
for doors to open – and reward
of bread and milk.

Prayer of a Countryman

When we are old, dear Lord, with hair turned grey
and wisdom's wrinkles line our agèd face,
let not affliction mar our latter day
and so prevent us joying in Thy grace.

For should the scourge of blindness close our eye
we should not see the rainbow of the flowers,
nor yet the changing cloud shapes of the sky,
the wheeling bats, and moths in twilight hours.

And should the curse of deafness be our lot,
how could we hear the vixen's thrilling call?
the hum of bees when days are bright and hot,
the hooting owl when night begins to fall?

How could we stir, if limbs were racked with pain,
to walk across the heath and through the wood?
or feel the stinging of November rain
and let the wind go whipping through the blood?

Let us not end our days in sad despair,
who, in our time, have all creation blessed,
but in life's garden breathe the evening air
and tend the soil, until it's time for rest.

MOURNING

The Farm Cat

A cat came down the lane
hobbling, but with dignity,
long-haired but battered
by weather and with age.

She sat on the paved path
in the cool Spring sunlight,
back to the West wind
ruffling through her fur.

She bent her head to the slab,
resigned by utter weariness
to a fleeting moment's comfort,
the brief warmth of grey stone.

We took her to the farm,
to the barn's scented shelter,
the comfort of dry straw,
her former kitten home.

What effort did it cost,
what strong determination,
to feebly drag her body
again along the lane?

We found her in the morning,
cushioned in mint and marjoram,
stretched in the April sunshine,
and honoured her request.

We let her die in peace
in the place that she had chosen:
her epitaph a human verse,
her dirge – a lone crow cawing.

Blackberrying

Blackberries – luscious, bittersweet,
like beads of polished jet clustered
on this September's cloaking hedge.
"Come with me now and harvest them,
ripe to be bottled, jellied, stewed
or, better still, to fragrance apple pies".

It's Sunday church, demanding child,
or visitors, or special lunch –
"You go – later perhaps I'll come".
"I find God in the fields amongst
damsel flies, bees, the rising lark –
His own creation. Come with me?" Too late –

The children grown, dispersed; the dog
watching me pick the fruit alone.
I see a figure climb the stile –
throat-catching silhouette and voice –
"Hello! … I thought I'd find you here …
where Daddy blackberried so long ago".

Last Post

I sit and watch you through the sick-bed night:
teeth in the bedside cup leave your face gaunt,
eyes are in-sunk, down-lidded from the light;
your poor old body needs a wash I fear,
and yet your breath is sweet … what shadows haunt
the slumbers of your ninety-second year?
what gone-ghosts does your struggling spirit meet?

Your lovely sisters? – young, but gone before –
mother and father, brothers, colleagues, friends?
in what frail fantasy your meetings soar?
Transparent hands clutch at the reins, the gear
of long-lost cavalry – shrivelled the lips that bend
to whisper daydreams in a French girl's ear;
today, at last, you ride to Calvary.

Night brings dismay, disturbance, duty dour –
the ebbing hours their sleep-lack lunacy –
you rise and, fumbling, wet upon the floor
and I, exhausted, cease to love, revere,
long for your final breath. Night brings despondency –
like you in Flanders so I know I hear
ominous rattle of approaching death.

You have known fear before: the Great War stench
of rotting comrades; the hours when you have sat
by Mother's death-bed – worse than mud-filled trench –
glad to escape to baby smiles and years
of homely ways; then your own small flat
and now the sheltered, heated bed-sit where
you've lately lived your Rip-van-Winkle days –

(with freshly-painted walls to make it bright
and hide the marks that previous tenants left).
Was it my strength that helped relieve your plight?
the day that I was ill – did not appear –
you could no more pretend, feeling bereft;
you are the baby that I once was, dear,
a kiss – and God knows when the heart-beats end.

In the Midst of Life

Death cups its hand like a cold stone bowl
or a hollowed hole in a stream-bed boulder
old as the fells:
holding the cool clear water of life,
glinting bright, bubbling with light
in a proffered palm;
and we drink with a deep unquenchable thirst
until hearts would burst, as if lips were dry,
the supply never end –
till we drown in the depths where the shadows lie,
our lives ephemeral, brittle and brief
as a dragonfly.

Set Aside

Snow clouds storm the dark north-east
above old fields that are set-aside:
where once you watched the springing wheat,
then rubbed the seed through winnowing thumb –
a score of skylarks lift against
dead blackness of the eye to come.

For threescore Autumns ploughing here
hessianed from the driving rain,
pained to the nerve in piercing wind –
yet heartened by high-hovering song,
and wintering sheep on neighbour's land
swelling with quickening of Spring.

You knew the weather breeders well
and country lore, from father's knee:
"If Candlemas Day be fair and bright
Winter will take another flight";
you knew the game, you played it tough –
taking your talents as your right.

Moss greens the ground where skylarks flock,
stubble bursts under booted feet –
but yours no more; your body sinks
through myriad memories left behind,
and who knows now what dreams you reap,
what plans lie dormant in your mind?

Soon, when night's dim hidden moon
mirrors the sun like octant glass,
you, with only your thoughts alive,

drift where the old fraternity
(crow-like in sombre mothballed black)
gathers ritualistically.

Packed to the door they whisper now
words that the parson dares not speak:
you were respected, feared, not loved;
so be it ... your creator guide
ploughed your last furrow to the end
and now has gently set aside.

20th Century Secrets

Uncomplicated clover grew,
for a smock-frocked girl of five,
in tall thick verges of Summer green
painted on blue;
cat's tail, fox tail and meadow softgrass
blurred with pollen, dark with secrets,
deep red clover ... and mauve ...and white!
honey-petalled, warm with scent.

In Lilliput grass the dreams are gone:
flattened, weird, grotesque,
the clover sprouts thalidomide flowers
forty years on;
the struggle for life is stunted and warped
by herbicides, pesticides – treated seed
food for the blue tits, unknowing and dead,
spread on a clutch of unhatched eggs.

Foot and Mouth Sunday

Stillness broods across the land –
sheep, wary, awaiting birth,
awaiting death;
even the lambs, silent, crouch
by dams unable to avert
this sword of Damocles.

Distance muffles the calling bells:
Come pray to God for He alone
can save you from impending doom.
It is not God who brings distress
but man's decade of waywardness.
Come raise your stock as God decreed
your children then may reap the seed.

Amorous pigeons clack their wings,
celandines gleam, woodpeckers drum
that Winter's gone;
but black smoke drifts from nearby hills,
pastures empty – first sign of death
for grieving Spring.

Eccleshall Churchyard

This is the second Autumn you have lain in this cold spot:
full eighteen months since we have left you resting here,
and yet I feel no strong emotion tearing me;
a loss? ah yes – a loss that feet no longer walk,
that heart no longer beats and eyes no longer see;
but in my hand I sense your warm and loving hand
and by my side a presence always there;
your spirit knows more than your eyes could ever see –
you are not lost.

Primrose Days

The primrose days are over,
the blown flowers gone
and the wind cold.

Joy in the light, bright breezes,
the dazzle of sun, is turned
to a raw chill.

"Come back, remembered faces!
Let me see you smile
in the sun's halo!"

"Ah, but we cannot return
when the flowers have been picked
and the river crossed".

Do not weep long

Do not weep long:
Death is a journey we are all
at some time called to make.
Life, the beginning
when we find companions for
the road we choose to take.

Some flit about -
ill-fated moths by starlight, caught
in deceptive flames of pain.

Fate gave me you,
trusted and loved companion; we
shall surely meet again.

MEMORIES

The Sledgers

You slide
in blobs of pink and blue
with sledging shrieks
down Winter's snowdrift slope.

Where do you live?
there are no houses near
and children have not
skidded down that hill
for many a year.

Had you worn grey
I would have said
that ghosts had come
to play.

The Seaside

Skipping and singing with delight –
a little ginger-headed mite
running with joy towards the sea.

Traffic Jam

A traffic cone stands at a place in the road
where a piano stool once stood ...
in the wink of an eye,
in a magical blink,
I sit upon the piano stool;
a piano appears
and I play with one finger;
with a benign Edwardian smile
my grandmother looks
from a heavy black frame –
a cap of dark curls,
high-throated black gown;
her father, in portly
Victorian dress,
looks jovially down –
the traffic moves on ...
the moment has gone.

Memories of a Bookworm

I remember Fairy Tales when I was very small,
read by Dad at bedtime as dusk began to fall:
princesses and ducklings and beanstalks very tall,
all conjured up by infant mind upon the bedroom wall.

Stories from the Classics came when I was still a child:
Odysseus and his sailors by siren songs beguiled;
Icarus, Persephone and Zeus in storm-clouds wild;
Bible-storied Sunday school of Jesus meek and mild.

We sauntered back from daily school – all chattering – until
the library loomed in Rowley Street ... with chins upon the sill
we eyed the books like treasure trove, made sure we had our fill
of all the books by Captain Johns and Angela Brazil.

Teenage years brought study books and opened wider doors
to views of France and Latin tales of Caesar's Gallic wars,
and spellbound hours with Shakespeare and poetry because
the lilt of music lifts their words until the spirit soars.

My adult years are passing fast and time is short – indeed
I fear there never will be days or hours enough to read
the books that I accumulate on mystery, space and creed,
or recommended books by friends whose intellect I heed.

Now must I praise librarians – devoted, patient, keen,
renewing, stamping, ordering fiction or fact – I mean
they even show us how to use the new computer screen!
Let's drink a toast – without their help where would we all
                                        have been?

January 1993

Incredibly that Spring the flowers came
a full month early!
After December cold – and thick hoar frost
of Christmas Day
cloaking the slopes of Chase enchantingly
as in old fairy tales –
the winds came with a sudden gusting warmth
straight from the South,
or from the West with whistling weirdness
and flooding rain;
yet under Winter's sodden brown I found
the buds of aconite
bursting like butterballs on trim green plates
of fronded leaves.
Startlingly white through creeping ivy hung
small snowdrop heads
and by subsiding waters of the stream
a celandine
bunched round by fat green buds – six weeks ahead
of normal years.
Like the old tale of Rose Red's strawberries,
under deep snow,
there seemed to be enchantment in the wind
that sudden Spring.

Summer's End in Long Leasow

My heart is in this field,
my soul in flowers that hang or hide
or spread their carpet-colours through the grass;
flamboyant foxgloves, secret moschatel,
chamomile, stitchwort and the alba rose,
bluebells and harebells, speedwell's sprinkled blue,
cream hogweed, meadowsweet and guelder rose,
purples of betony, hard-iron, clover, vetch,
pink campion, willowherb, the Roman rose;
search out St. John's wort, dainty nipplewort
and fourteen clumps of precious primroses –
you see, I count them all!

We've picnicked in this field
with tiny children by the paddling brook,
and searched for coloured stones and rabbit holes,
feathers and fox's 'job', badger latrines,
(which little William called "a treasure hunt");
and walked four dogs in turn – tolling our years –
hare-chasing, muck-rolling, careless themselves of time;
calf-crèche encircled tight by guardian cows
from sheeting rain; and, in an early dawn,
gossamer sea of dandelion clocks.

This field's enhanced my life
and bears me on a tide of memories –
carthorses nibbling by the wooden stile
and fertilizing ground for mushroom hoards!
magical days there've been when I have seen
vixen and cubs through a monocular,

– no longer there – nor swathes of scented hay
but plastic black-bagged grass with sickly smell;
no barn owl beats the air in falling dusk –
yet dragonflies still zoom through August's heat
and searching swallows swoop at summer's end;
sunsets still glow, soft breezes stir the grass …
time now to turn again for home, and so
depart as swallows do.

Should we have Buskers in the Market Square?

The Italianate piazza of our modern County Town
spreads like sand between the buildings; strangers saunter
   up and down.

Gone the bustle I remember (and remembering, I mourn)
of the noisy market traders setting up their stalls at dawn.

Cheerful neighbour jostling neighbour, friends with cries of
   recognition,
while a jerky barrel-organ loudly played in competition.

Long before grandparents' childhood – drovers, tinkers,
   carter's load,
gaunt-faced men with hurdy-gurdies squelched along the
   muddy road.

Sheridan and Izaak Walton, Rupert, Bess – their spirits come –
entertained by bawdy comic, shawm and sackbut,
   pipe and drum.

Ethelfleda on her island, in the marshy mists of founding,
and her bard in flickering firelight with his ancient tales
   astounding.

Now with flute, guitar and cello, welcome to the old
   Shire Hall! –
woolly hats for catching pennies – "Thanks Staffordians,
   one and all!"